AMAZING ANIMALS

EMUS

BY MARI BOLTE

CREATIVE EDUCATION • CREATIVE PAPERBACKS

Published by Creative Education
and Creative Paperbacks
P.O. Box 227, Mankato, Minnesota 56002
Creative Education and Creative Paperbacks
are imprints of The Creative Company
www.thecreativecompany.us

Design by The Design Lab
Production by Blue Design
Art direction by Graham Morgan

Images by Getty Images/Colin Baker, 13, imageBROKER/David & Micha Sheldon, 17, imageBROKER/Jurgen & Christine Sohns,18, Jami Tarris, 14, John Carnemolla, 6; Pexels/JARMAN Gill, 5, Maheera Kulsoom, 21; Unsplash/David Clode, 2, Melissa Keizer, cover, 1, Trevor McKinnon, 23; Wikimedia Commons/Auckland Museum Collections, 8, Dominic Sherony, 10, Henrik Gronvold, 20, JJ Harrison, 9, Roger Culos, 15, Yi ZHANG, 11

Cataloging-in-Publication data is available from the Library of Congress.
Library Binding ISBN: 9798895810545
Paperback ISBN: 9798896800071
eBook ISBN: 9798895811801
LCCN: 2025011188

Printed in China

Table of Contents

Life on the Ground	4
Top Speed	6
Big Birds	8
Time for a Snack	12
Nesting	14
Forever Grounded	18
An Emu Tale	22
Read More	24
Websites	24
Index	24

Emus are large, flightless birds with long legs and necks. They are the second-largest living bird in the world, after ostriches. They are the biggest bird in Australia. It is the only place they can be found in the wild.

Emus can make loud, booming roars that can reach up to 1.2 miles (2 kilometers) away.

Long legs help emus run fast. They can reach speeds of up to 31 miles (50 kilometers) per hour. Emus are also very strong. Three toes with sharp, curved claws make an emu kick deadly.

Emus can jump 7 feet (2 meters) straight into the air.

Emus can be tan, gray, or brown. Unlike other birds, their feathers are not waterproof.

An average emu stands more than 5 feet (1.5 m) tall. Females weigh more than males, around 120 pounds (54.4 kilograms). Shaggy feathers are not good for flying, but they fluff up to keep emus warm.

shaggy long and messy

People also farm emus. Emu meat, eggs, leather, feathers, and oil are used around the world.

Emus can be found around most of Australia, from open plains to sandy deserts. Once, there were several species. Today, the common emu is the only one left. There are as many as 725,000 wild adult emus living in Australia.

species a group of animals with similar characteristics

Finding food is an emu's biggest job. Emus can travel for hundreds of miles to find food and water. Both plants and bugs are on the menu. As emus wander from one place to another, they poop out seeds, spreading them around to grow.

Emus have fat stores that help them get by during lean times.

Female emus lay two to three clutches of eggs during the season.

Emus breed once a year. Males build nests out of grass and sticks on the ground. Females lay 5 to 15 eggs in the nest. Then, the females leave forever. Males sit on the eggs until they hatch.

clutch a nest of eggs or a brood of chicks

Chicks are born after about eight weeks. Their striped feathers help them hide from predators. At six months, the birds are fully grown. They may stay with their father for up to 18 months, though.

One emu egg can weigh as much as a dozen chicken eggs.

Emus are so strong because they are the only bird with calf muscles. They can run for a long time without getting tired. The same muscles that help them run make them good swimmers.

Emu legs are covered in scales. The scales are protection against predators' sharp teeth and claws.

Other flightless birds include ostriches, rheas, cassowaries, and kiwis.

Emus have wings, but they are too small to help them fly. But emus don't need to fly. They don't need to **migrate** to find safe places to nest. If a predator gets too close, emus can kick them or run away. Emus are unique!

migrate to move from one place to another

An Emu Tale

During the coldest and wettest time of the year, native people looked up and saw the Emu in the Sky. This shape is created by dark spots in the Milky Way. It makes its first appearance at the beginning of emu mating season. By June or July, the emu's legs have disappeared. It looks like it is sitting on a nest. In August, it looks more like an emu egg. By November, the emu completely disappears.

Read More

Nilsen, Genevieve. *Emu Chicks*. Minneapolis: Jump!, 2022.

Rice, Jamie. *Emu or Ostrich?* Minneapolis: Jump!, 2023.

Riggs, Kate. *Ostriches*. Mankato, MN: Creative Education and Creative Paperbacks, 2023.

Websites

Britannica Kids: Emu
https://kids.britannica.com/kids/article/emu/390741
Learn about these huge flightless birds.

San Diego Wildlife Explorers: Emu
https://sdzwildlifeexplorers.org/animals/emu
Read fun and interesting facts about emus.

Note: Every effort has been made to ensure that the websites listed above are suitable for children, that they have educational value, and that they contain no inappropriate material. However, because of the nature of the Internet, it is impossible to guarantee that these sites will remain active indefinitely or that their contents will not be altered.

Index

breeding, 15
constellation, 22
diet, 12
feathers, 8, 11, 16
legs, 4, 7, 19, 22
necks, 4
size, 4, 8
species, 11
speed, 7
toes, 7
wings, 20